AF472081

FAQ's of Faith

Printed in the United States of America.

Cover Photograph by Bill Shick

To Beau—
With all my heart . . .
As always.

Now faith is the assurance of things hoped for,
the conviction of things not seen.
Hebrews 1:1

And without faith it is impossible to please Him,
for whoever would draw near to God must believe that
He exists and that he rewards those who seek Him.
Hebrews 11:6

Trust in the Lord with all your heart,
and do not lean on your own understanding.
In all your ways acknowledge Him,
and He will make straight your paths.
Proverbs 3:5-6

And those who know Your name put their trust in You,
for You, O Lord, have not forsaken those who seek You.
Psalm 9:10

The Lord is my strength and my shield;
in Him my Heart trusts, and I am helped;
my heart exults, and with my song
I give thanks to Him.
Psalm 28:7

FAQ's of Faith

Table of Contents

Give me, O Lord, a steadfast heart, which no unworthy affection may drag downwards. Give me an unconquered heart, which no tribulation can wear out. Give me an upright heart, which no unworthy purpose may tempt aside.

(Thomas Aquinas)

Who Is God & What Is He to Me?

God is Everything to us!

No one else can be so much for and to us -- anytime ... all the time ... anything ... everything!

If we let Him, God can, and will, satisfy our every need. His love can overcome every fear, put our doubting to rest, comfort our broken hearts, and overcome loneliness.

Our stubbornness ... our willful pride is the only thing preventing us from enjoying His love and presence. God is always right beside us ... waiting for us to accept His love and all He can do for us.

And my God will fully supply your every need according to His glorious riches in the Messiah Jesus.
Philippians 4:19 ISV

Without fail, God is there for us – to help, comfort, guide, encourage, protect, strengthen, provide for, love, and care for and about us.

And there is salvation in and through no one else, for there is no other name under heaven given among men by and in which we must be saved.
Acts 4:12

For I am the Lord your God, Who takes hold of your right hand and says to you, do not fear; I will help you.
Isaiah 41:13

Without doubt, the mightiest thought the mind can entertain is the thought of God, and the weightiest word in any language is its word for God.
(A.W. Tozer)

"God" is the name used to describe the three Divine Beings Who share a common nature:
The Father, the Son, and the Holy Spirit

The Father = the Ultimate Authority

- Lord Almighty

The Son = Jesus, the Christ

- God revealed in human form
- The Way, the Truth, the Life
- Reconciled us to the Father

The Holy Spirit = God's Spirit in us

- Comforter, Counselor, Truth
- Takes our supplications to the Father
- The Power that works in and through us

He shall call upon Me, and I will answer him; I will be with him in trouble, I will deliver him and honor him.
Psalm 91:15

... Who bears our burdens and carries us day by day, even the God Who is our salvation.
Psalm 68:19

[God] disarmed the principalities and powers that were ranged against us and made a bold display and public example of them, in triumphing over them in Him and in it [the cross].
Colossians 2:15 AMP

Who is a God like You, Who forgives iniquity and passes over the transgression...? He retains not His anger forever, because He delights in mercy and loving-kindness. He will again have compassion on us; He will subdue and tread underfoot our iniquities. You will cast all our sins into the depths of the sea. You will show Your faithfulness and perform the sure promise to Jacob and loving-kindness and mercy to Abraham, as You have sworn to our fathers from the days of old.
Micah 7:18-20

The Lord is my Strength and my [impenetrable] Shield; my heart trusts in, relies on, and confidently leans on Him, and I am helped; There my heart greatly rejoices, and with my song will I praise Him.
Psalm 28:7 AMP

Into Your hands I commit my spirit; You have redeemed me, O Lord, the God of truth and faithfulness.
Psalm 31:5

... the God of your hope
Romans 15:13

He blessed Abram saying, "Blessed be Abram by God Most High, Creator of heaven and earth.
Genesis 14:19

... He is my Refuge and my Fortress, my God;
on Him I lean and rely, and in Him I trust!
Psalm 91:2

What eye has not seen and ear has not heard and has not entered into the heart of man, [all that] God has prepared (made and keeps ready) for those who love Him [who hold Him in affectionate reverence, promptly obeying Him and gratefully recognizing the benefits He has bestowed].
1 Corinthians 2:9 AMP

Find rest, O my soul, in God alone; my hope comes from Him.
Psalm 62:5

The Lord is my Rock, my Fortress, and my Deliverer; my God, my keen and firm Strength in Whom I will trust and take refuge, my Shield, and the Horn of my salvation, My High Tower.
Psalm 18:2

He saved us, not because of any works of righteousness that we had done, but because of His own pity and mercy, by the cleansing of the new birth and renewing of the Holy Spirit.
Titus 3:5

God Provides ...

Psalm 23

Relationship -	The Lord is my Shepherd
Supply -	I shall not want
Rest -	He makes me to lie down in green pastures
Refreshment -	He leads me beside still waters
Healing -	He restoreth my soul
Guidance -	He leads me in paths of righteousness
Purpose -	For His name's sake
Testing -	Even though I walk through the valley of the shadow of death
Protection -	I will fear no evil
Faithfulness -	For Thou art with me
Discipline -	Thy rod and Thy staff, they comfort me
Hope -	Thou preparest a table before me in the presence of my enemies
Consecration-	Thou annointest my head with oil
Abundance -	My cup runneth over
Blessing -	Surely goodness and mercy shall follow me all the days of my life
Security -	and I will dwell in the house of the Lord
Eternity -	Forever

(Source Unknown)

Why Should I Care About God?!

God created every one of us and knows everything about us...the good and the bad, our strengths and our weaknesses … all that separated us from Him ... our every thought.

It is impossible to hide anything from God.

But in spite of our weaknesses, God loves us; and because of our weaknesses God set in motion His plan for us to be reconciled to Him. This He did before time began then carried that plan out at just the right time ...

... when He sent His Son, our Savior, to die in our place, to take the punishment we deserve, and provide for us a way back to Him.

Jesus took the punishment for our sins and spent three days in Hades, separated from everything good before being raised from the pit. Isn't that alone, a good enough reason to care about God?!

In the beginning God (prepared, formed, fashioned, and) created the heavens and the earth. God said, Let Us [Father, Son, and Holy Spirit] make mankind in Our image, after Our likeness, and let them have complete authority over the fish of the sea, the birds of the air, the [tame] beasts, and over all of the earth, and over everything that creeps upon the earth. So God created man in His own image, in the image and likeness of God He created him; male and female He created them.
Genesis 1:1, 26, 27 AMP

… just as Jonah was in the belly of the sea creature, so will the Son of Man be three days and three nights in the heart of the earth.
Matthew 12:40

[God] disarmed the principalities and powers that were ranged against us and made a bold display and public example of them, in triumphing over them in Him {Christ} and in it [the cross].
Colossians 2:15

And there is salvation in and through no one else, for there is no other name under heaven given among men by and in which we must be saved.
Acts 4:12

{We} are being guarded (garrisoned) by God's power through [your] faith [till you fully inherit that final] salvation that is ready to be revealed [for you] in the last time.
1 Peter 1:5 AMP

"I have loved you with an everlasting love;
I have drawn you with loving-kindness."
Jeremiah 31:3

I have told you these things, so that in Me you may have [perfect] peace and confidence. In the world you have tribulation and trials and distress and frustration; but be of good cheer [take courage; be confident, certain, undaunted]! For I have overcome the world. [I have deprived it of power to harm you and have conquered it for you.]
John 16:33 AMP

For God so loved the world that he gave his one and only Son, that whoever believes in him shall not perish but have eternal life. For God did not send his Son into the world to condemn the world, but to save the world through Him.
John 3:16-17 NIV

For God did not appoint us to suffer wrath but to receive salvation through our Lord Jesus Christ.
1 Thessalonians 5:9 NIV

What Will God Do For Me?

God provides everything we need in order to be complete, content, saved...

God wants only what is best for us. Remember though, that what is best for us is not necessarily what will bring us immediate happiness in our earthly life, but what will lead us to eternal salvation.

Knowing that God is watching over us and is in control, and that His plan for us is for our good, should be the source of our joy.

Many plans are in a man's mind,
but it is the Lord's purpose for him that will stand.
Proverbs 19:21

For I know the thoughts and plans that I have for you, says the Lord, thoughts and plans for welfare and peace and not for evil, to give you hope in your final outcome.
Jeremiah 29:11

When we seek to know God, He reveals Himself to us. God IS the gift we receive. That which we seek ... eternal life of knowing God ... that is His gift to us.

It is because of the Lord's mercy and loving-kindness that we are not consumed, because His [tender] compassions fail not. The Lord is good to those who wait hopefully and expectantly for Him, to those who seek Him [inquire of and for Him and require Him by right of necessity and on the authority of God's word].
Lamentations 3:22, 25 AMP

The Lord will give strength to His people;
the Lord will bless His people with peace.
Psalm 29:11

The Lord your God is in the midst of you, a Mighty One, a Savior [Who saves]! He will rejoice over you with joy; He will rest [in silent satisfaction] and in His love He will be silent and make no mention [of past sins, or even recall them]; He will exult over you with singing.
Zephaniah 3:17 AMP

...What eye has not seen and ear has not heard and has not entered into the heart of man, [all that] God has prepared (made and keeps ready) for those who love Him [who hold Him in affectionate reverence, promptly obeying Him and gratefully recognizing the benefits He has bestowed].
1 Corinthians 2:9 AMP

{He, through His} power that is at work within us, is able to [carry out His purpose and] do superabundantly, far over and above all that we [dare] ask or think [infinitely beyond our highest prayers, desires, thoughts, hopes, or dreams]
Ephesians 3:20 AMP

Now the Lord is the Spirit, and where the Spirit of the Lord is, there is liberty (emancipation from bondage, freedom).
2 Corinthians 3:17 AMP

If we [freely] admit that we have sinned and confess our sins, He is faithful and just (true to His own nature and promises) and will forgive our sins [dismiss our lawlessness and continuously] cleanse us from all unrighteousness [everything not in conformity to His will in purpose, thought, and action].
1 John 1:9 AMP

See what [an incredible] quality of love the Father has given (shown, bestowed on) us, that we should [be permitted to] be named and called and counted the children of God!
1 John 3:1 AMP

... God's love has been poured out in our hearts through the Holy Spirit Who has been given to us.
Romans 5:5

What's In It for Me?

The benefits of being a child of God far outweigh what God requires of us. If we never received anything in this life, eternal salvation in the next life should be more than enough to motivate us to believe.

Because God wants us to succeed, He has blessed us with power over Satan and the pain of sin in this life, peace (even in times of trouble), comfort for our hearts in any situation, and His constant abiding Presence.

Nobody and nothing can separate us from Him. How's that for security?!

It is a privilege to be able to serve Him ... and, doing what He asks of us, is part of the benefits we receive as His children.

However, it is being in right standing with God that should be our main goal and focus. Pleasing Him should be our deepest desire.

"[After all] the kingdom of God is not a matter of [getting the] food and drink [one likes], but instead it is righteousness (that state which makes a person acceptable to God) and [heart] peace and joy in the Holy Spirit."
(Romans 14:17 AMP)

For you shall go out [from spiritual exile caused by sin and evil into the homeland] with joy and be led forth [by your Leader, the Lord Himself, and His Word] with peace;
Isaiah 55:12 AMP

Until now you have asked nothing in my name. Ask, and you will receive, that your joy may be full.
John 16:24b

... For I consider that the sufferings of this present time (this present life) are not worth being compared with the glory that is about to be revealed to us and is in us and for us and conferred on us!
Romans 8:18 AMP

You will guard him and keep him in perfect and constant peace whose mind [both its inclination and character] is stayed on You, because he commits himself to You, leans on You, and hopes confidently in You.
Isaiah 26:3

For both He Who sanctifies [making men holy] and those who are sanctified all have one [Father], for this reason He {Jesus} is not ashamed to call them brethren.
Hebrews 2:11

Now the mind of the flesh [which is sense and reason without the Holy Spirit] is death [death that comprises all the miseries arising from sin, both here and hereafter]. But the mind {led by} of the [Holy] spirit is life and [soul] peace [both now and forever].
Romans 8:6 AMP

... in the coming ages He might show the immeasurable riches of His grace in kindness toward us in Christ Jesus. For by grace you have been saved through faith. And this is not your own doing; it is the gift of God ...
Ephesians 2:7-8 ESV

The steps of a [good] man are directed and established by the Lord when He delights in his way [and He busies Himself with his every step]. Though he falls, he shall not be utterly cast down, for the Lord grasps his hand in support and upholds him.
Psalm 37:23-24 AMP

Therefore do not be anxious, saying, 'What shall we eat?' or 'What shall we drink?' or 'What shall we wear?' [33] But seek first the kingdom of God and his righteousness, and all these things will be added to you.
Matthew 6:31, 33

How Do I Know God Is Even There?

Evidence of God's Presence is in everything we see, hear, smell, and feel.

You can't see the air you breathe, but it's definitely there! You can feel the air ... see evidence of its presence.

The Lord is always near ... closer than the breath we breathe. As long as we walk in the Light and keep His commandments, God will be with us ... He will dwell in us. (John 14:23)

Because he set his love on Me, therefore I will save him; I will set him [securely] on high, because he knows My name [he confidently trusts and relies on Me, knowing I will never abandon him, no, never].
(Psalm 91:14)

God will always make Himself known to those who seek Him.

You will seek Me and find Me when you search for Me with all your heart.
Jeremiah 29:13 ISV

Close your eyes and look with the eyes of your heart ... you'll see Him!

For the eyes of the Lord are upon the righteous (those who are upright and in right standing with God), and His ears are attentive to their prayer.
1 Peter 3:12a

And I will betroth you to Me forever; yes, I will betroth you to Me in righteousness and justice, in steadfast love and in mercy.
Hosea 2:19

Faith is the assurance (the confirmation, the title deed) of things [we] hope for, being the proof of things [we] do not see and the conviction of their reality [faith perceiving as real fact what is not revealed to the senses].
Hebrews 11:1 AMP

But without faith it is impossible to please Him, for he who comes to God must believe that He is {exists}, and that He is a rewarder of those who diligently seek Him.
Hebrews 11:6

For we walk by faith, not by sight.
2 Corinthians 5:7

And behold, I am with you and will keep (watch over you with care, take notice of) you wherever you may go. ... for I will not leave you until I have done all of which I have told you.
Genesis 28:15 AMP

Let your gentleness be evident to all. The Lord is near.
Philippians 4:5

Without having seen Him, you love Him; though you do not [even] now see Him, you believe in Him and exult and thrill with inexpressible and glorious (triumphant, heavenly) joy.
1 Peter 1:8 AMP

Blessed be the Lord, who bears our burdens and carries us day by day, even the God Who is our salvation.
Psalm 68:19

And the Lord said, My Presence shall go with you, and I will give you rest.
Exodus 33:14

Where could I go from Your Spirit?
Or where could I flee from Your presence?
Psalm 139:7

How Do I "Find" God and Get Faith?

Faith doesn't just "happen".

Faith comes from hearing the Word of God. The more knowledge of God we acquire, the more we understand the awesomeness of God; the more we comprehend about God, the stronger our faith will become.

Living by faith is a lifestyle ... not something you "try". You have to commit to your beliefs when it's easy and when it's difficult.

If your faith isn't as strong as you want it to be, the way to change that is to learn ... know more about all God has done for us and His promises for now and our future ... the only way to learn more about God is by reading His Word.

You will seek Me ... and find Me when you search for Me with all your heart.
Jeremiah 29:13

... If you seek Him [inquiring for and of Him, craving Him as your soul's first necessity], He will be found by you.
2 Chronicles 15:2

So that they should seek God in the hope that they might feel {grope} after Him and find Him, although He is not far from each one of us.
Acts 17:27

But when He, the Spirit of Truth (the Truth-giving Spirit) comes, He will guide you into all the Truth (the whole, full Truth). For He will not speak His own message [on His own authority]; but He will tell whatever He hears [from the Father; He will give the message that has been given to Him], and He will announce and declare to you the things that are to come [that will happen in the future].
John 16:13 AMP

Faith comes by hearing, and hearing through the word of Christ.
Romans 10:17 ESV

Meditate on these things; give yourself entirely to them, that your progress may be evident to all. Take heed to yourself and to the doctrine. Continue in them, for in doing this you will save both yourself and those who hear you.
1 Timothy 4:15-16 NKJB

A scoffer seeks Wisdom in vain [for his very attitude blinds and deafens him to it], but knowledge is easy to him who [being teachable] understands.
Proverbs 14:6 AMP

All Scripture is given by inspiration of God, and is profitable for doctrine, for reproof, for correction, for instruction in righteousness, that the man of God may be complete, thoroughly equipped for every good work.
2 Timothy 3:16-17 NKJB

The reverent and worshipful fear of the Lord is the beginning and the principal and choice part of knowledge [its starting point and its essence]; but fools despise skillful and godly Wisdom, instruction, and discipline.
Proverbs 1:7 AMP

But if from there you will seek (inquire for and require as necessity) the Lord your God, you will find Him if you [truly] seek Him with all your heart [and mind] and soul and life.
Deuteronomy 4:29

A common mistake we make is that we look for God in places where we ourselves wish to find him, yet even in the physical reality this is a complete failure. For example, if you lost your car keys, you would not search where you want to search you would search where you must in order to find them."
(Criss Jami)

God Doesn't Understand What My Life is Like!

Since God does not walk in the flesh with us in this earthly life and we can't see Him, we tend to forget something very important ...

The Father never walked the earth, but the Son did! And He was tempted, most notably, in Matthew 4:1-10. But throughout Jesus' entire ministry, Satan pursued Him ... to the very end.

The people insisted on "signs" to prove who He was, others wanted to make Him their earthly king, and at the end, He was taunted by the people while He hung on the cross.

He knows what it feels like to experience sorrow, pain, and frustration. Yet He sinned not.

Jesus was betrayed by a man in His inner circle – a friend; He was beaten, spat upon, whipped, mocked and killed in the most demoralizing manner for nothing He had done … to save us.

And because the Father, Son and Holy Spirit share a common nature and mind, God does indeed know and understand our troubles in this life.

He Himself has suffered in being tempted, He is able to run to the cry of those who are being tempted.
Hebrews 3:18

For we do not have a High Priest Who is unable to understand and sympathize and have a shared feeling with our weaknesses and infirmities and liability to the assaults of temptation, but One Who has been tempted in every respect as we are, yet without sinning.
Hebrews 4:15

For I know the thoughts and plans that I have for you, says the Lord, thoughts and plans for welfare and peace and not for evil, to give you hope in your final outcome.
Jeremiah 29:11

[God] disarmed the principalities and powers that were ranged against us and made a bold display and public example of them, in triumphing over them in Him and in it [the cross].
Colossians 2:15 AMP

... as the Scripture says, What eye has not seen and ear has not heard and has not entered into the heart of man, [all that] God has prepared (made and keeps ready) for those who love Him [who hold Him in affectionate reverence, promptly obeying Him and gratefully recognizing the benefits He has bestowed].
1 Corinthians 2:9 AMP

You have kept count of my wanderings. Put my tears in your bottle– have not You recorded them in Your book?
Psalm 56:8 ISV

Who is a God like you, who pardons sin and forgives the transgression of the remnant of his inheritance? You do not stay angry forever but delight to show mercy. You will again have compassion on us; you will tread our sins underfoot and hurl all our iniquities into the depths of the sea.
Micah 7:18-19

My child, you worry too much. I've got this, remember?!
Love, God

I Can't Understand the Bible!

There is so much to read and learn in the Bible; we can sometimes feel overwhelmed at all there is to learn.

But God doesn't require that we know all that He has revealed to us all at once; In fact, it is impossible for our human mind to perfectly know and understand all that is written for us.

It is the process ... the lifelong journey, the race run with endurance that God looks at ... hearts that persevere.

When we approach our studying with a heart for earnestly learning about God we will find Him.

So I say to you, Ask and keep on asking and it shall be given you;
seek and keep on seeking and you shall find; knock and keep
knocking and the door shall be opened to you.
Luke 11:9

God does not compare our progress to that of others' so neither should we. The progress others make may be more or less than what God knows we can do. Jesus is the example to emulate ... the standard to strive toward.

... for whoever would draw near to God must believe that He exists
and that He rewards those who seek Him.
Hebrews 11:6

If any of you lacks wisdom, let him ask of God, who gives to all
liberally and without reproach, and it will be given to him.
James 1:5 NKJV

... knowledge comes easily to the discerning
Proverbs 14:6b

His divine power has given to us all things that pertain to life and godliness, through the knowledge of Him who called us by glory and virtue …
2 Peter 1:3

For that which is known about God is evident to them and made plain in their inner consciousness, because God [Himself] has shown it to them.
Romans 1:19

I [the Lord] will instruct you and teach you in the way you should go; I will counsel you with My eye upon you.
Psalm 32:8

He leads the humble in what is right, and the humble He teaches His way.
Psalm 25:9

... if you seek the Lord your God, you will find Him if you seek Him with all your heart and with all your soul.
Deuteronomy 4:29b

… that according to the riches of His glory He may grant you to be strengthened with power through His Spirit in your inner being, so that Christ may dwell in your hearts through faith -- that you, being rooted and grounded in love, may have strength to comprehend with all the saints what is the breadth and length and height and depth, and to know the love of Christ that surpasses knowledge, that you may be filled with all the fullness of God.
Ephesians 3:16-19

But whenever a person turns to the Lord, the veil is removed. As all of us reflect the glory of the Lord with unveiled faces, we are becoming more like him with ever-increasing glory by the Lord's Spirit.
2 Corinthians 3:16,18

How Do I Know I'm On the Right Track?

The only way to know for certain that we are doing what God wants is by knowing what God wants; the only way to know what God wants from us is to read His Word. The Bible is the only place we can find God's instruction and guidance to us.

If we do what we think God wants us to do without actually confirming it in the Bible we will get off track. Even with the best of intentions, our hearts may lead us astray.

There is a way that seems right to a man and appears straight before him, but at the end of it is the way of death.
Proverbs 16:25 AMP

So we need to continually "check" and prove our beliefs and actions against God's Word. Study to show ourselves approved (2 Timothy 3:16).

All we need to know is in the Scriptures ... so read them!

"But Jesus replied to them, You are wrong because you know neither the Scriptures nor God's power."
Matthew 22:29

This is how we can be sure that we have come to know Him: if we continually keep His commandments. The person who says, "I have come to know Him," but does not continually keep His commandments is a liar, and the truth has no place in that person. But whoever continually keeps His commandments is the kind of person in whom God's love has truly been perfected.
1 John 2:3-5 ISV

But whoever lives by the truth comes into the light, so that it may be seen plainly that what they have done has been done in the sight of God.
John 3:21 NIV

No one who remains in union with Him keeps on sinning. The one who keeps on sinning hasn't seen Him or known Him. The person who practices righteousness is righteous, just as the Messiah is righteous. No one who has been born from God practices sin, because God's seed abides in him. Indeed, he cannot go on sinning, because he has been born from God.
1 John 3:6, 9 NIV

You will show me the path of life; in Your presence is fullness of joy, at Your right hand there are pleasures forevermore.
Psalm 16:11

No one has ever seen God; but if we love one another, God lives in us and His love is made complete in us.
1 John 4:12 NIV

He who believes in the Son of God [who adheres to, trusts in, and relies on Him] has the testimony [possesses this divine attestation] within himself. He who does not believe God [in this way] has made Him out to be and represented Him as a liar, because he has not believed (put his faith in, adhered to, and relied on) the evidence (the testimony) that God has borne regarding His Son. And this is that testimony (that evidence): God gave us eternal life, and this life is in His Son. He who possesses the Son has that life; he who does not possess the Son of God does not have that life. I write this to you who believe in (adhere to, trust in, and rely on) the name of the Son of God [in the peculiar services and blessings conferred by Him on men], so that you may know [with settled and absolute knowledge] that you [already] have life, yes, eternal life.
1 John 5:10-13 AMP

... he who carries out His purposes in life abides (remains) forever.
1 John 2:17b AMP

What Do I Have To Do?

The objective of worshipping and obeying God is not to do as little as possible. God is not pleased with half-hearted service to Him.

God wants complete devotion from His people. He longs to be gracious to us, to show loving-kindness to us, but He will not force His way into our lives.

Those whom God is seeking are humble and have a broken heart for their sin and who revere His commands (Isaiah 66:2b).

God has the power to do anything and everything He wants. However, what He desires from us is a humble submissive heart ... and He will not forcibly take it.

The one thing we must willingly give to God ... is our hearts.

And you shall love the Lord your God out of and with your whole heart and out of and with all your soul (your life) and out of and with all your mind (with your faculty of thought and your moral understanding) and out of and with all your strength. This is the first and principal commandment.
Mark 12:30

Do not let gracious love and truth leave you. Bind them around you neck, write them on the tablet of your heart.
Proverbs 3:3 ISV

My command is this: Love each other as I have loved you.
John 15:12

Having purified your souls by your obedience to the truth for a sincere brotherly love, love one another earnestly from a pure heart.
1 Peter 1:22 ESV

If you declare with your mouth that Jesus is Lord, and believe in your heart that God raised Him from the dead, you will be saved. For one believes with his heart and is justified, and declares with his mouth and is saved.
Romans 10:9-10 (ISV)

... make every effort to supplement your faith with virtue, and virtue with knowledge, and knowledge with self-control, and self-control with steadfastness, and steadfastness with godliness, and godliness with brotherly affection, and brotherly affection with love.
2 Peter 1:5-7 ESV

My sacrifice to God is a broken spirit; a broken and a contrite heart, such, O God, You will not despise.
Psalm 51:17

For the commandments, "You shall not commit adultery, You shall not murder, You shall not steal, You shall not covet," and any other commandment, are summed up in this word: "You shall love your neighbor as yourself." Love does no wrong to a neighbor; therefore love is the fulfilling of the law.
Romans 13:9-10

... Repent and be baptized, every one of you, in the name of Jesus Christ for the forgiveness of sins; and you shall receive the gift of the Holy Spirit.
Acts 2:38

Commit to the Lord whatever you do, and He will establish your plans.
Proverbs 16:3 NIV

The real beauty is in the heart. The real treasure is in heaven.
The true salvation is in God;
The real joy is in serving God with all your heart and sincerity.
(Innah Delos Angeles)

God Doesn't Care What Happens To Me!

God is out of our "sight" ... we can't see Him with our physical eyes so we sometimes let Him slip out of our minds. But rest assured, we are never out of God's sight and we are always on His mind.

God validates every one of the worries and pain that we experience. Take comfort in knowing that God knows our problems and sees our tears. He hears the pain in our voice.

Earthly parents care for and about their children ... even more, God cares for and about His children. The difference is that God knows, without a doubt, what is best for us and has the power to make it so!

Keep in mind that what we want and think is best for us may not actually be. We see only a narrow and limited view of the physical. God knows the whole picture ... physical and spiritual from the beginning to the end.

He wants what is best for us and will make it happen ... if we let Him.

Trust Him.

Casting the whole of your care on Him, for He cares for you affectionately and cares about you watchfully.
1 Peter 5:7

Cast your burden on the Lord [releasing the weight of it] and He will sustain you; He will never allow the [consistently] righteous to be moved (made to slip, fall, or fail).
Psalm 55:22 AMP

When I look at Your heavens, the work of Your fingers, the moon and the stars, which You have set in place, what is man that You are mindful of him, and the son of man that You care for him?
Psalm 8:3-4

And I will ask the Father, and He will give you another Comforter, that He may remain with you forever -- The Spirit of Truth, Whom the world cannot receive (welcome, take to its heart), because it does not see Him or know and recognize Him. But you know and recognize Him; for He lives with you [constantly] and will be in you.
John 14:16-17

But [even] the very hairs of your head are all numbered. Do not be struck with fear or seized by alarm ...
Luke 12:7a

You have kept count of my wanderings. Put my tears in your bottle--have not You recorded them in Your book?
Psalm 56:8

Who is a God like You, Who forgives iniquity and passes over the transgression of the remnant of His heritage? He retains not His anger forever, because He delights in mercy and loving-kindness. He will again have compassion on us; He will subdue and tread underfoot our iniquities. You will cast all our sins into the depths of the sea.
Micah 7:18-19 AMP

And therefore the Lord [earnestly] waits [expecting, looking, and longing] to be gracious to you; and therefore He lifts Himself up, that He may have mercy on you and show loving-kindness to you. For the Lord is a God of justice. Blessed (happy, fortunate, to be envied) are all those who [earnestly] wait for Him, who expect and look and long for Him [for His victory, His favor, His love, His peace, His joy, and His matchless, unbroken companionship]!
Isaiah 30:18 AMP

For He will command His angels concerning you to guard you in all your ways. On their hands they will bear you up, lest you strike your foot against a stone.
Psalm 91:11-12 ESV

As one whom his mother comforts, so will I comfort you.
Isaiah 66:13a

Do I Get To Keep Doing All the Fun Stuff?

This "fun stuff" ... does it satisfy you? Is it what makes you feel relaxed and content? Are your body and mind strengthened afterwards?

Or could it be that you are actually searching for something that feels just out of reach ... for something to fill a deep-felt need?

What if the "fun stuff" isn't the answer?! If you were to stop partying, drinking, etc., wouldn't you then be free to pursue things you've always wanted to do, but were afraid to try … maybe thought you weren't good enough, smart enough, strong enough to do?

You would have the freedom to do what you've only dreamed and wished but never imagined you were capable of doing ... important, meaningful things!

You can do all things through Christ Who strengthens you. Commit all your work to God and you will be successful.

I {Paul} therefore ... appeal to and beg you to walk (lead a life) worthy of the [divine] calling to which you have been called [with behavior that is a credit to the summons to God's service, Living as becomes you] with complete lowliness of mind (humility) and meekness (unselfishness, gentleness, mildness), with patience, bearing with one another and making allowances because you love one another.
Ephesians 4:1-2 AMP

Now the Lord is the Spirit, and where the Spirit of the Lord is, there is liberty (emancipation from bondage, freedom).
2 Corinthians 3:17 AMP

Strip yourselves of your former nature ... which characterized your previous manner of life ... And be constantly renewed in the Spirit of your mind ... And put on the new nature (...) created in God's image...
Ephesians 4:22-24 AMP

Looking away [from all that will distract] to Jesus, Who is the Leader and the Source of our faith [giving the first incentive for our belief] and is also its Finisher [bringing it to maturity and perfection]. He, for the joy [of obtaining the prize] that was set before Him, endured the cross, despising and ignoring the shame, and is now seated at the right hand of the throne of God.
Hebrews 12:2 AMP

For everything that is in the world – the desire for fleshly gratification, the desire for possessions, and worldly arrogance – is not from the Father but is from the world.
1 John 2:16 ISV

Do not be deceived, my beloved brothers. Every good gift and every perfect gift is from above, coming down from the Father of lights with whom there is no variation or shadow due to change.
James 1:16-17

The thief comes only in order to steal and kill and destroy. I came that they may have and enjoy life, and have it in abundance (to the full, till it overflows).
John 10:10 AMP

And do not turn aside after empty things that cannot profit or deliver, for they are empty.
1 Samuel 12:21

Sin will take you where you didn't plan to go;
It will keep you there longer than you planned to stay;
And it will cost you more than you intended to pay!
(James L. Nicodem)

I Can't Do Everything the Bible Says To Do!

"Don't want to" or "can't"? Think about it … because they are two different issues and involve completely different hearts. "Don't want to" entails making excuses to get out of having to do something you don't want to do; "Can't" is another thing and God addresses that matter. You need to be honest with yourself before you can move on.

God's love for you does not hinge on whether you achieve perfection. God is looking for people who *strive* for perfection ... who are dedicated and devoted ... faithful to Him.

We must have a desire to know and please God ... to be who and what He wants us to be.

Our motivation in the decisions we make should not be from fear of being caught doing something wrong but rather, from a desire to bring joy to God when we do His will.

Apart from God we can do nothing ... we can accomplish nothing on our own strength.

But give your all to pleasing Him and God will give you whatever talent and strength you need to accomplish His purpose for you.

God is looking for people that seek Him … hearts that desire to please Him … faith that waits for Him.

... you are of God [you belong to Him] and have [already defeated and overcome them [the agents of the antichrist], because He Who lives in you is greater (mightier) than he who is in the world.
1 John 4:4 AMP

I am the Vine; you are the branches. Whoever lives in Me and I in him bears much (abundant) fruit. However, apart from Me [cut off from vital union with Me] you can do nothing.
John 15:5 AMP

For with God nothing is ever impossible and no word from God shall be without power or impossible of fulfillment.
Luke 1:37

... continuously be transformed by the renewing of your minds so that you may be able to determine what God's will is – what is proper, pleasing, and perfect.
Romans 12:2 ISV

We are assured and know that [God being a partner in their labor] all things work together and are [fitting into a plan] for good to and for those who love the Lord and are called according to [His] design and purpose.
Romans 8:28 AMP

I have strength for all things in Christ Who empowers me [I am ready for anything and equal to anything through Him Who infuses inner strength into me; I am self-sufficient in Christ's sufficiency].
Philippians 4:13 AMP

Roll your works upon the Lord [commit and trust them wholly to Him; He will cause your thoughts to become agreeable to His will, and] so shall your plans be established and succeed.
Proverbs 16:3 AMP

He has showed you, O man, what is good. And what does the Lord require of you? To act justly and to love mercy and to walk humbly with your God.
Micah 6:8

Then He told all of them, "If anyone wants to come with Me, he must deny himself, pick up his cross every day, and follow Me continuously … "
Luke 9:23

Do the best you can until you know better.
Then, when you know better, do better.
(Maya Angelow)

What About All the Bad Stuff I've Done?

Welcome to the human race!
We have all done things we knew we shouldn't do and wish we hadn't.

But God didn't send His Son to die on the cross for people who were already perfect and didn't need Him.

In His infinite wisdom and love, God made a way for us to have life with Him ... now and for eternity --

That is our confident expectation ... Hope!

... their sins and law-breaking I will remember no more.
Hebrews 10:17

We must recognize our depravity before we can repent of it. But we can't let the guilt of our past cripple us as we look forward to our future.

Christ bore our guilt so we wouldn't have to. We need to admit and confess our sins, learn from our mistakes and move on ... and thank God for His mercy and grace!

He personally bore our sins in His [own] body on the tree [as on an altar and offered Himself on it], that we might die (cease to exist) to sin and live to righteousness. By His wounds you have been healed.
1 Peter 2:24 AMP

Now the Lord is the Spirit, and where the Spirit of the Lord is, there is liberty (emancipation from bondage, freedom).
2 Corinthians 3:17 AMP

For He has rescued us from the dominion of darkness and brought us into the kingdom of the Son He loves, in whom we have redemption, the forgiveness of sins.
Colossians 1:13-14

... but one thing I do [it is my one aspiration]: forgetting what lies behind and straining forward to what lies ahead, I press on toward the goal to win the [supreme and heavenly] prize to which God in Christ Jesus is calling us upward.
Philippians 3:13-14 AMP

For thus said the Lord God, the Holy One of Israel: In returning [to Me] and resting [in Me] you shall be saved; in quietness and in [trusting] confidence shall be your strength.
Isaiah 30:15a AMP

The Lord does not delay and is not tardy or slow about what He promises, according to some people's conception of slowness, but He is long-suffering (extraordinarily patient) toward you, not desiring that any should perish, but that all should turn to repentance.
2 Peter 3:9 ISV

If we [freely] admit that we have sinned and confess our sins, He is faithful and just (true to His own nature and promises) and will forgive our sins [dismiss our lawlessness] and [continuously] cleanse us from all unrighteousness [everything not in conformity to His will in purpose, thought, and action].
1 John 1:9 AMP

For if you forgive people their trespasses [their reckless and willful sins, leaving them, letting them go, and giving up resentment], your heavenly Father will also forgive you.
Matthew 6:14 AMP

The Lord is close to those who are of a broken heart and saves such as are crushed with sorrow for sin and are humbly and thoroughly penitent.
Psalm 34:18

The Lord your God is in your midst, a mighty one who will save; He will rejoice over you with gladness; He will quiet you by His love; He will exult over you with loud singing.
Zephaniah 3:17

There Are Too Many Rules to Follow!

1. Love God.
Is that too much to ask in return for all the blessings of this life that God provides AND eternal salvation?

2. Love one another.
That's too much for you to handle? Don't you want others to treat you kindly, be compassionate towards you, love you? You're somebody else's "another" ... so you need to love "one another" as well.

This is My commandment: that you love one another [just] as I have loved you.
John 15:12 AMP

Isn't that what we would all like from others toward us?

All that God wants us to do is "life" to those who believe and obey. Everything is for our good/benefit and, by extension, for those we love ... and will never harm anyone else in the process.

I give you a new commandment:
that you should love one another. Just as I have loved you, so you too should love one another. By this shall all [men] know that you are My disciples, if you love one another [if you keep on showing love among yourselves].
John 13:34-35 AMP

For the whole law is fulfilled in one word: "You shall love your neighbor as yourself."
Galatians 5:14

… and may the Lord make you increase and abound in love for one another and for all, as we do for you
1 Thessalonians 3:12

Love is patient, love is kind. It does not envy, it does not boast, it is not proud. It does not dishonor others, it is not self-seeking, it is not easily angered, it keeps no record of wrongs. Love does not delight in evil but rejoices with the truth.
1 Corinthians 13:4-6 NIV

Above all things have intense and unfailing love for one another, for love covers a multitude of sins [forgives and disregards the offenses of others].
1 Peter 4:8

... do all according to the law... Turn not from it ..., that you may prosper wherever you go. ... meditate on it {God's Word} day and night, ... for then you shall make your way prosperous, and you shall deal wisely and have good success.
Joshua 1:7-8

... whatever is true, whatever is honorable, whatever is just, whatever is pure, whatever is lovely, whatever is commendable, if there is any excellence, if there is anything worthy of praise, think about these things.
Philippians 4:8 ESV

And this is His order (His command, His injunction); that we should believe in (put our faith and trust in and adhere to and rely on) the name of His Son Jesus Christ (the Messiah), and that we should love one another, just as He has commanded us.
1 John 3:23 AMP

For the whole Law is summarized in a single statement:
"You must love your neighbor as yourself."
Galatians 5:14 ISV

And let us consider and give continuous, attentive care to watching over one another, studying how we may stir up (stimulate and incite) to love and helpful deeds and noble activity.
Hebrews 10:24 AMP

Who Is Jesus, and What Is He to Me?

Jesus is God in human form, the Son. Emmanuel … God with us.

He was sent from the Father to reconcile us to Him after we separated ourselves from Him with our sin. He is our Savior. He rescued us!

Jesus lived a perfect life ... completely sinless.

Then, once and for all of us, He bore our guilt and shame from all of our sin so we wouldn't have to.

He left His home in Heaven with His Father to live and die on this earth ... because He loves us.

Jesus is our Savior, our Shepherd, our Healer, our Light ... our very Life.

Through Jesus, we have hope beyond death.

He is the exact likeness of the unseen;
He is the Firstborn of all creation.
Colossians 1:15

Behold the virgin will become pregnant and give birth to a Son, and they shall call His name Emmanuel - which, when translated, means, God with us.
Matthew 1:23

... the prince of the world is coming. And he has no claim on Me.
John 14:30

No matter what storms are raging all around, you'll stand firm if you stand on Jesus' love.
(Charles Stanley)

I have told you these things, so that in Me you may have [perfect] peace and confidence. In the world you have tribulation and trials and distress and frustration; but be of good cheer [take courage; be confident, certain, undaunted]! For I have overcome the world. [I have deprived it of power to harm you and have conquered it for you.]
John 16:33 AMP

While we were yet in weakness [powerless to help ourselves] at the fitting time Christ died for (in behalf of] the ungodly.
Romans 5:6

And He is the Head of all rule and authority [of every angelic principality and power].
Colossians 2:10b AMP

... Christ, Who is the image and Likeness of God.
2 Corinthians 4:4b

I am He that liveth, and was dead; and behold I am alive for evermore, Amen; and have the keys of hell and of death.
Revelation 1:18

"... I am the Alpha and the Omega, the Beginning and the End.
Revelation 21:6b

I am the Good Shepherd.
The Good Shepherd lays down His life for the sheep.
John 10:11

Christ, our Passover [Lamb], has been sacrificed.
1 Corinthians 5:7b AMP

... the Lamb of God, Who takes away the sin of the world.
John 1:29

I am the Light of the world. He who follows Me will not be walking in the dark, but will have the Light which is Life.
John 8:12

... we have a great High Priest Who has [already] ascended and passed through the heavens, Jesus the Son of God, let us hold fast our confession [of faith in Him]. {We have a High Priest Who is able} to understand and sympathize with our weaknesses, ... One Who has been tempted in every respect as we are, yet without sinning.
Hebrews 4:14-15

... He is the God-appointed and God-ordained Judge of the living and the dead.
Acts 10:42

Christ [is] the Power of God and the Wisdom of God.
1 Corinthians 1:24 AMP

... I am the Way and the Truth, and the Life. No one comes to the Father except through Me.
John 14:6

In Him was Life, and the Life was the Light of men. And the Light shines on in the darkness, for the darkness has never overpowered it [put it out or absorbed it or appropriated it, and is unreceptive to it].
John 1:4-5 AMP

I am the true Vine, and My Father is the Vinedresser {Gardener}. Dwell in Me, and I will dwell in you ... I am the Vine; you are the branches. ... apart from Me you can do nothing.
John 15:1, 4, 5

For to us a Child is born, to us a Son is given; and the government shall be upon His shoulder, and His name shall be called Wonderful Counselor, Mighty God, Everlasting Father, Prince of Peace.
Isaiah 9:6

... He is always living to make petition to God and intercede with Him and intervenes for them {those who come to God through Him}.
Hebrews 7:25b

... "I am the Bread of Life. Whoever comes to Me will never go hungry, and whoever believes in Me will never be thirsty.
John 6:35

But the free gift is not like the trespass. For if many died through one man's {Adam's} trespass, much more have the grace of God and the free gift by the grace of that one man Jesus Christ abounded for many. And the free gift is not like the result of that one man's sin. For the judgment following one trespass brought condemnation, but the free gift following many trespasses brought justification.
Romans 5:15-16 ESV

For because He Himself [in His humanity] has suffered in being tempted (tested and tried), He is able [immediately] to run to the cry of (assist, relieve) those who are being tempted and tested and tried [and who therefore are being exposed to suffering].
Hebrews 2:18 AMP

The Son is the radiance of God's glory and the exact representation of His being, sustaining all things by His powerful word. After He had provided purification for sins, He sat down at the right hand of the Majesty in heaven. So He became as much superior to the angels as the name He has inherited is superior to theirs. For to which of the angels did God ever say, "You are My Son; today I have become Your Father"? Or again, "I will be His Father, and He will be my Son"? And again, when God brings His firstborn into the world, He says, "Let all God's angels worship Him." In speaking of the angels He says, "He makes His angels spirits, and His servants flames of fire." But about the Son He says, "Your throne, O God, will last for ever and ever; a scepter of justice will be the scepter of Your kingdom.
Hebrews 1:3-8

For this reason Christ is the mediator of a new covenant, that those who are called may receive the promised eternal inheritance—now that he has died as a ransom to set them free from the sins committed under the first covenant.
Hebrews 9:15

What Is a Holy Spirit and What Is It For?

God spoke to the people through prophets ... the people rejected Him.

Then He sent His only Son to teach and be an example ... the people rejected and killed Him.

Christ promised not to leave us alone when He returned to heaven. So, our Father sent His Holy Spirit to be another Comforter, Counselor, Helper, Intercessor, Strengthener to us.

The Holy Spirit was sent by the Father … *our* Father to guide us, to help us become more like our Father; He dwells in God's children helping us prepare to meet our Father face to face. He prepares even our prayers to be received by our Father.

For those who choose to reject the Holy Spirit, there will not be another ... no more warnings after the Holy Spirit's time with us.

Don't waste your only opportunity.

Or do you suppose that the Scripture is speaking to no purpose that says, the Spirit Who He has caused to dwell in us yearns over us and He yearns for the Spirit [to be welcome] with a jealous love? But He gives us more and more grace (power of the Holy Spirit, to meet this evil tendency and all others fully).
James 4:5-6a AMP

When you believed, you were marked in Him {Christ} with a seal, the promised Holy Spirit, Who is a deposit guaranteeing our inheritance until the redemption of those who are God’s possession –to the praise of His glory.
Ephesians 1:13b-14 NIV

For who knows a person’s thoughts except their own spirit within them? In the same way no one knows the thoughts of God except the Spirit of God.
1 Corinthians 2:11 AMP

For who knows a person's thoughts except their own spirit within them? In the same way no one knows the thoughts of God except the Spirit of God.
1 Corinthians 2:11 AMP

But the Comforter (Counselor, Helper, Intercessor, Advocate, Strengthener, Standby), the Holy Spirit, Whom the Father will send in My {Jesus'} name [in My place, to represent Me and act on My behalf], He will teach you all things.
John 14:26 AMP

And if the Spirit of Him Who raised up Jesus from the dead dwells in you [then] He who raised up Christ Jesus from the dead will also restore your mortal (short-lived, perishable) bodies through His Spirit Who dwells in you. If you live according to the flesh you will surely die; putting to death the [evil] deeds of the body, you shall live forever. For all who are led by the Spirit are sons of God. But [the Spirit] you have now received is not a spirit of slavery (bondage) to put you once again in bondage to fear, but you have received the Spirit of adoption [producing son-ship] in [the bliss of] which we cry, Abba, Father!
Romans 8:11, 13 AMP

He {the Father} will give you another Comforter (...), that He may remain with you forever – The Spirit of Truth, ... lives with you [constantly] and will be in you.
John 14:16-17 AMP

... the [Holy] Spirit comes to our aid and bears us up in our weakness; for we do not know what prayer to offer nor how to offer it worthily as we ought, but the Spirit Himself goes to meet our supplication and pleads on our behalf ...
Romans 8:26 AMP

The Spirit-filled life is not a special, deluxe edition of Christianity. It is part and parcel of the total plan of God for His people.
(A.W. Tozer)

Who Are God's People?

The child of God, in addition to having complete faith that God exists, loves the Lord ...with complete heart, soul, mind and strength. (Mark 12:30).

Those who believe and walk and live habitually guided by the Holy Spirit conducting themselves righteously are God's people; Not just willingly being, but choosing to be transformed into what and who God wants them to be, instead of being conformed to the world.

Children of God stand out from the world; they are different, because they choose to be and are happy to be known for their uniqueness.

Conduct yourselves properly (honorably, righteously) among the Gentiles, so that, although they may slander you as evildoers, they may by witnessing your good deeds [come to] glorify God in the day of inspection [when God shall look upon you wanderers as a pastor or shepherd looks over his flock].
1 Peter 2:12 AMP

Do you not know that your body is the temple (the very sanctuary) of the Holy Spirit Who lives within you, Whom you have received [as a Gift] from God? You are not your own, you were bought with a price [purchased with a preciousness and paid for, made His own]. So then, honor God and bring glory to Him in your body.
1 Corinthians 6:19-20 AMP

If you live in Me [abide vitally united to Me] and My words remain in you and continue to live in your hearts, ask whatever you will, and it shall be done for you. When you bear (produce) much fruit, My Father is honored and glorified, and you show and prove yourselves to be true followers of Mine.
John 15:7-8 AMP

… live a life worthy of the calling you have received. Be completely humble and gentle; be patient, bearing with one another in love.
Ephesians 4:1-2

For we are fellow workmen (joint promoters, laborers together) with and for God; you are God's garden and vineyard and field under cultivation, [you are] God's building.
1 Corinthians 3:9 AMP

... this is the man to whom I will look and have regard: he who is humble and of a broken or wounded spirit, and who trembles at My word and reveres My commands.
Isaiah 66:2b

But if we walk in the Light, as He is in the Light, we have fellowship with one another, and the blood of Jesus His Son cleanses us from all sin.
1 John 1:7 ESV

Whoever believes and is baptized will be saved, but whoever does not believe will be condemned.
Mark 16:16

If anyone is in Christ, he is a new creation; the old has gone, the new has come.
2 Corinthians 5:17

Do everything without grumbling or arguing, So that you may become blameless and pure, "children of God without fault in a warped and crooked generation." Then you will shine among them like stars in the sky as you hold firmly to the word of life.
Philippians 2:14-16a

Clothe yourselves therefore, as God's own chosen ones, purified and holy and well-beloved tenderhearted pity and mercy, kind feeling, a lowly opinion of yourselves, gentle ways,.
Colossians 3:12

Change for the Better

The life God wants us to leave behind is so contaminated with sin that it does us harm by even being near it!

The consequences of living a life of sin affect us and the people we love in so many ways ... ways that don't even occur to us when we are presented with choices.

Relationships are damaged, trust destroyed, lines of communication severed, hearts broken – all caused by choices we make to invite and allow sin into our lives.

Putting off the old man in order to imitate Christ and please the Father is the only way to right wrongs and start the healing process.

And knowing that the people in your life have the same life-goal that you do, knowing they are striving to be the people God wants them to be, share the same hope, and because they love as Christ commanded and want what is best for you ... that makes all the difference in the world in our relationships and how we live our lives..

Beloved, we are now God's children; it is not yet disclosed what we shall be, but we know that when He comes and is manifested, we shall resemble and be like Him, for we shall see Him just as He is. And everyone who has this hope on Him cleanses himself just as He is pure.
1 John 3:2-3

For [you can look back now and] observe what this same godly sorrow has done for you and produced in you; what eagerness and earnest care to explain and clear yourselves …
2 Corinthians 7:11

But in a great house there are not only vessels of gold and silver, but also of wood and earthenware, and some for honorable and noble [use] and some for menial and ignoble [use]. So whoever cleanses himself [from what is ignoble and unclean, who separates himself from contact with contaminating and corrupting influences] will [then himself] be a vessel set apart and useful for honorable and noble purposes, consecrated and profitable to the Master, fit and ready for any good work.
2 Timothy 2:20-21 AMP

And all of us, as with unveiled face, continued to behold as in a mirror the glory of the Lord, are constantly being transfigured into His very own image in ever increasing splendor and from one degree of glory to another; from the Lord the Spirit.
2 Corinthians 3:18 NKJV

Any branch in Me that does not bear fruit [that stops bearing] He cuts away (trims off, takes away); and He cleanses and repeatedly prunes every branch that continues to bear fruit, to make it bear more and richer and more excellent fruit.
John 15:2 AMP

Train yourself toward godliness. For physical training is of some value (useful for a little), but godliness (spiritual training) is useful and of value in everything and in every way, for it holds promise for the present life and also for the life which is to come.
1 Timothy 4:7b-8 AMP

For the time that is past already suffices for doing what the Gentiles like to do –living [as you have done] in shameless, insolent wantonness, in lustful desires, drunkenness, reveling, drinking bouts and abominable, lawless idolatries. They are astonished and think it very queer that you do not now run hand in hand with them in the same excesses of dissipation, and they abuse [you]. But they will have to give an account to Him Who is ready to judge and pass sentence on the living and the dead.
1 Peter 4:3-5

Who's the Enemy?

The devil wrestles with God,
and the field of battle is the human heart.
(Feodor Dostoelski)

In Scripture Satan is referred to as the devil, the evil one, the author of all evil, the prince of darkness, a murderer, the adversary, the prince of this world, the god of this world, the father of lies, the destroyer, the oppressor.

The goal of Satan is to destroy as many of God's people as he can. There's no rhyme or reason other than that he is pure evil and hates everything good.

Don't kid yourself ... The devil is real!

And he will stop at nothing to distract you from your goal of one day being with God for eternity. He distorts the truth, manipulates situations to frustrate you, and anything else he thinks will throw you off course.

The most effective way to destroy God's people is to confuse them, steal their knowledge of God. Because without knowledge there is no understanding; without understanding we are unable to know God, His promises to us, and how to please Him.

My people are destroyed for lack of knowledge.
Hosea 4:6

The fear of the Lord is the beginning of knowledge;
fools despise wisdom and instruction.
Proverbs 1:7

The fear of the Lord is the beginning of wisdom, and the knowledge
of the Holy One is insight.
Proverbs 9:10

For the god of this world has blinded the unbelievers' minds [that they should not discern the truth], preventing them from seeing the illuminating light of the Gospel of the glory of Christ (the Messiah), Who is the image and likeness of God.
2 Corinthians 4:4 AMP

Now the Spirit expressly says that in later times some will depart from the faith by devoting themselves to deceitful spirits and teachings of demons, through the insincerity of liars whose consciences are seared
1 Timothy 4:1-2 AMP

... we have not ceased to pray and make request for you, that you may be filled with the full knowledge of His will in all spiritual wisdom [in comprehensive insight into the ways and purposes of God] and in understanding and discernment of spiritual things – That you may walk in a manner worthy of the Lord, fully pleasing to Him and desiring to please Him in all things, bearing fruit in every good work and steadily growing and increasing in and by the knowledge of God.
Colossians 1:9-10

He was a murderer from the beginning and does not stand in the truth, because there is no truth in him. When he speaks a falsehood, he speaks what is natural to him, for he is a liar [himself] and the father of lies and of all that is false.
John 8:44

The Lord asked Satan, "Where have you come from?" In response, Satan answered the Lord, "From wandering all over the earth and walking back and forth throughout it."
Job 1:7 AMP

The devil has only the power to entice us, not the power to coerce us.
(Gary Henry)

Hang In There!

Whatever age you are now ... did you imagine you would get here so quickly? Time seems to have flown by in the blink of an eye!

At the time it seemed like you would never make it through the problems you were experiencing; but whether the problems have been resolved or continue to this day ... you didn't die from them. You felt like giving up, but would turning your back on God really help?

Leaving the Lord won't make things any easier; in fact, you would be more lonely and would have absolutely no help in this life, and no hope for a better life for eternity. But you know that already; it's just hard to hear over the din and see through the fog ...

So close your eyes and live by faith. Let the eyes of your heart see with eternity in sight and be guided by the Holy Spirit.

By your steadfastness and patient endurance you shall win the true life of your souls.
Luke 21:19

Strive to enter by the narrow door, for many, I tell you, will seek to enter and will not be able.
Luke 13:24 ESV

And let us not lose heart and grow weary and faint in acting nobly and doing right, for in due time and at the appointed season we shall reap, if we do not loosen and relax our courage and faint.
Galatians 6:9

Be earnest and unwearied and steadfast in your prayer [life], being [both] alert and intent in [your praying] with thanksgiving.
Colossians 4:2 AMP

Do not, therefore, fling away your fearless confidence for it carries a great and glorious compensation of reward. For you have need of steadfast patience and endurance, so that you may perform and fully accomplish the will of God, and thus receive and carry away [and enjoy to the full] what is promised.
Hebrews 10:35-36

Just think of Him Who endured {Jesus} from sinners such grievous opposition and bitter hostility against Himself [reckon up and consider it all in comparison with your trials], so that you may not grow weary or exhausted, losing heart and relaxing and fainting in your minds.
Hebrews 12:3 AMP

Just hold on to what you have until I come. I will give authority over the nations to the person who overcomes and continues to do what I've commanded to the end.
Revelation 2:25-26

The thoughts of the diligent tend only to pleasantness, but everyone who is impatient and hasty hastens only to want.
Proverbs 21:5

Whoever does not persevere and carry his own cross and come after (follow) Me cannot be My disciple.
Luke 14:27 AMP

So keep up your courage, men, for I have faith (complete confidence) in God that it will be exactly as it was told me.
Acts 27:25

Therefore, my dear brothers, be steadfast, unmovable, always excelling in the work of the Lord, because you know that the work that you do for the Lord isn't wasted.
1 Corinthians 15:58 ISV

Withstand him {Satan}; be firm in faith ... And after you have suffered a little while, the God of all grace, Who has called you to His eternal glory in Christ Jesus, will Himself complete you and make you what you ought to be, establish and ground you securely, and strengthen and settle you.
1 Peter 5:9-10

So let us seize and hold fast and retain without wavering the hope we cherish and confess and our acknowledgment of it, for He Who promised is reliable (sure) and faithful to His word.
Hebrews 10:23 AMP

We are hard pressed on every side, yet not crushed; we are perplexed, but not in despair; persecuted, but not forsaken; struck down, but not destroyed; always carrying about in the body the dying of the Lord Jesus Christ, that the life of Jesus also may be manifested in our body.
2 Corinthians 4:8-10

If you faint in the day of adversity, your strength is small. Deliver those who are drawn away to death, and those who totter to the slaughter, hold them back [from their doom].
Proverbs 24:10-11 AMP

Therefore, since through God's mercy we have this ministry, we do not lose heart.
2 Corinthians 4:1 NIV

I have told you these things, so that in Me you may have [perfect] peace and confidence ... For I have overcome the world.
John 16:33a AMP

When a strong man, fully armed, guards his own dwelling {home}, his belongings are undisturbed [his property is at peace and is secured].
Luke 11:2 AMP

And my God will liberally supply (fill to the full) your every need according to His riches in glory in Christ Jesus.
Philippians 4:19

For He will repay everyone according to what that person has done: eternal life to those who strive for glory, honor, and immortality by patiently doing good; but wrath and fury for those who in their selfish pride refuse to believe the truth and practice wickedness instead. There will be suffering and anguish for every human being who practices doing evil ... But there will be glory, honor, and peace for everyone who practices doing good.
Romans 2:7-10

[You should] be exceedingly glad on this account, though now for a little while you may be distressed by trials and suffer temptations, so that [the genuineness] of your faith may be tested, [your faith] which is infinitely more precious than the perishable gold which is tested and purified by fire. [This proving of your faith is intended] to redound to [your] praise and glory and honor when Jesus Christ (the Messiah, the Anointed One) is revealed.
1 Peter 1:6-7 AMP

And do not grieve the Holy Spirit of God [do not offend or vex or sadden Him], by Whom you were sealed (marked, branded as God*s own, secured) for the day of redemption (of final deliverance through Christ from evil and the consequences of sin).
Ephesians 4:30

Be faithful, even to the point of death, and I will give you life as your victor's crown.
Revelation 2:10

Permanence, perseverance, and persistence in spite of all obstacles, discouragements, and impossibilities: It is this that in all things distinguishes the strong soul from the weak.
(Thomas Carlyle)

THE ARMOR OF GOD ...

BELT OF TRUTH	JN. 17:17
BREASTPLATE OF RIGHTEOUSNESS/ INTEGRITY	2 TIM. 3:16-17
SHOES OF PREPARATION FROM PEACE	COL. 1:5
SHIELD OF FAITH	ROM. 10:17
HELMET OF SALVATION	2 TIM. 3:15
SWORD OF THE HOLY SPIRIT (THE WORD OF GOD)	EPH. 6:17

When a strong man, fully armed, guards his own house,
his possessions are safe.
Luke 11:21

Thoughts to Remember

Those whose hearts are filled with the greatest adoration of God are those whose minds see most clearly who He really is.
(Gary Henry)

One is given strength to bear what happens to one, but not the 101 different things that *might* happen.
(C.S. Lewis)

We can't do God's job and He won't do what He told us to do.
(Tim Young)

God will do His work in us if we will do our work in Him.
(Wilson Adams)

Through Christ we are God's success story.
(Rickie Jenkins)

God will not violate our freedom. He stands silently in the background of our minds, waiting for us to remember that He is with us.
(Sarah Young)

Out of trials come blessings, otherwise hidden.
(Unknown)

Elements of Great Faith:
Properly Directed ... Penitent ... Reverent ... Persistent ... Humble
(Rickie Jenkins)

When Christ's Presence is the focal point of your consciousness, all the pieces of your life fall into place.
(Sarah Young)

"Lust" means "I must have it at once." Spiritual lust causes me to demand an answer from God, instead of seeking God Himself Who gives the answer.
(Oswald Chambers)

God looks for persistence - rather than perfection - in our walk with Him.
(Sarah Young)

You can't have hope unless you think about what God has promised you.
(Wilson Adams)

God comforts us not to make us comfortable but to make us comforters.
(John Henry Jowett)

Being right with God hinges on a right reaction to His Son.
(Jacob Hudgins)

Our spiritual growth and faith has an effect on those close to us. We can encourage and comfort them with our faith.
(Rickie Jenkins)

God has gifted us with amazing freedom, including the ability to choose the focal point of our minds.
(Sarah Young)

We long for more than we have because we were made for more than our hearts can reach right now.
(Gary Henry)

No situation is hopeless when God is involved, because He is the God of Hope!
(Tim Young)

I will say of the Lord, He is my Refuge and my Fortress, my God; on Him I lean and rely, and in Him I [confidently] trust!
Psalm 91:2 AMP

Now the Lord is the Spirit, and where the Lord's Spirit is, there is freedom.
2 Corinthians 3:17

In Him and through faith in Him we may approach God with freedom and confidence.
Ephesians 3:12

Through faith in God we can trust Him. Trusting that God is in control gives us freedom. Freedom from sin, worry, anxiety, trying to control things that are impossible for us to control ... allows us to enjoy the peace that God offers His children.

Let God be God; He will do His part; and you can focus on being a better you ... the “you” He knows you can be.

Acknowledgements

Becky, for always being there and for your kind honesty ...
I cherish our time together!

Lauren, you're always there to lift me up.
Thanks for being my friend and Sis.

Rickie & Jody, for listening and loving ...
thank you!

Tim & Anna Lee, for opening your hearts and home
and showing me how to open my heart and mind ...
thank you always!

www.ingramcontent.com/pod-product-compliance
Ingram Content Group UK Ltd.
Pitfield, Milton Keynes, MK11 3LW, UK
UKHW041914190726
13854UKWH00003B/1246

9 780359 132812